TONIGHT I WANT TO LIVE AND

Ryan Norman is a writer from Beverley. His work has appeared in *The Rialto*, *bath magg*, *Poetry Wales*, and elsewhere. In 2019, he received an MA in Creative Writing Poetry from UEA. He works as an editor in London.

PRAISE for *Tonight I Want to Live and*

The poems in *Tonight I Want to Live and* take the full range of that open-ended conjunction – they play with possibility and place, from the body to the spiritual, the gym to the garden, where hornets make a nest. Norman writes, in one poem, that 'My thoughts are trapped // like water in stone'. This pamphlet is a wonderful well-spring, tapped; full of dams and tributaries and sudden, brilliant flourishings.

— Seán Hewitt

This pamphlet offers an intense search for meaning in the boxing gym and beyond, delving into the rituals, repetitions and sheer hard work it takes to truly meet 'the body and the flower within that body'. Whether contemplating physical or emotional pain, solitude or relationship, the things of the world or what we do to our own and others' bodies, these deeply thoughtful poems invite us to join them in their meditations.

— Meryl Pugh

Sometimes you come across poems which seem to open up a brand-new, undefiled territory. It's the very distinct world that the poems in this pamphlet emerge from that gives them their freshness. The body training, the built body as an extension of the self, the damaged body, the body boxing; and alongside all of that, a powerful depiction of the body as the home of the isolated inwardly searching voice of the poems. There's a peculiar intimacy here, as well as an unusual combination of machismo and sensitivity. These poems come at you from a completely unexpected angle, like a disguised punch.

— Mark Waldron

Ryan Norman's poems initially read as if they are about the body – and the way that they communicate physical pain lands like a punch – but what's most impressive about this pamphlet debut is how the life of the senses in these poems is also the life of the mind, and what I admire most is how these poems speak to us, very affectingly, about the mind, about loneliness and about fellow feeling. This is auspicious work and an achievement on its own terms.

— John McAuliffe

CONTENTS

ISBN: 978-1-916938-26-7

Cover designed by Aaron Kent

Edited and Typeset by Aaron Kent

Broken Sleep Books Ltd
PO BOX 102
Llandysul
SA44 9BG

Tonight I Want to Live and

Ryan Norman

Broken Sleep Books

HEART

A boxing glove, I can tell you, will never expose
the essential matter of a cheek. Not the blood

or mother who waited in her car, but the decision,
minutes ago, to lace up gloves. A sledgehammer

failed to find this conviction in the walls
of my house. You opened my cheek, found

what? They say there's a firefly below a cup
at the centre of the earth, lighting the glass

like a secret. Could you pick up that cup?
What will you tell my mother, still waiting

in her car, when she learns it's our fault
all the streetlights have gone out?

LODE

the boxer pummelling the bag
is burrowing down
to the flower in his core

with every smack
sweat is flung from his face as the heavy bag
jangles from its chain

he is tearing down to the piece of himself
that will allow him to crunch the bones of another

in a fight pain can go unnoticed
like blood in a tsunami

but during training the body
of your opponent is present
in your mind

the body and the flower within that body

you're confronted with your capacity to break a man
to snap his rib with the speed of your glove
split his jaw
like a wishbone

it takes a particular piece of soul
to wreck a body like this

but in the ring a fighter is numb to any humanity
that is not
an exchange of fists

which is its own language

so often the fighter is barely aware
they're digging down to the truth of themselves

I was exposed as a coward after turning my back
on a sparring partner

this shame is still unfurling between my ribs

it was impossible for me to do anything other than jab at my brother
who once fought on in a white shirt
bloodied and sweaty as a tablecloth
soaked by wine and rain

perhaps then if the fighter wants to learn about their self

the flower is never more present than in the ring

the soul torn open like a wound

blood sodden leaves in the flesh

LIFTED

after a minor ACL tear
in the gym
there are solar flares of pain in my knee
azure winds on my patella

the bar is cold on my shoulders as I return it to the rack
my face still dry

today is not a day
to train
but to appreciate what I've built

I return to the changing room
remove my shirt

and the mirror a validation of the years I've spent below metal

bones that hardened to stone with the effort of every squat

the muscles around them drenched in agony

this is not a vanity

you build something for years and tell me you're not proud

tell me your body doesn't now express the burning fucking passion
        you have for life

they'd have you believe that every man in here is inwardly on his knees

that the foam of the bench is torn out and its fabric

is flapping open like skin

/

in the wooden light of the pub the smell of beer
wafts
pierced by the clink of glasses

I know the concrete floor of the cellar

the beermat I twirl in my fingers

and below my shirt
the shape of my body defines me

my work ethic expressed
through the fabric stretched
over my back

and again the chairs scrape the floor

into another barrel the hammer smashes the tap

/

what I've learned from the gym is repetition

how performing the same motions day after day
is a current
shaping a stone

the gym floor as the bed of a river

our effort drawing the water

swirling the sediment

/

there are men who compete in physique competitions
stand on stage in colourful shorts

all forced smiles and dry bodies
skin stretched over their muscle like raisins

I don't pity them

they're not suffering; they're displaying years
of work

the work just happens to be their bodies

and there's always a danger of fragility

but I trust them to regulate their emotions like canals

/

because the hatred is only brief I promise

the main thing is the deepened weight with which you carry yourself
in the cold light of your office

dust moving in and out of the blades
and outside
just as many birds as usual

/

and what I've learned is that pain
is a way to press into the self

to learn if you can endure the scream
of another squat

if you have the bravery
to break open the light at your core

the closer you get to this truth of your strength

the brighter the agony spread out to your body becomes

each hoist of the barbell one layer of flesh closer

to the orb in your chest

I learned I can do it

and into life I took that knowledge like a key

/

following the knee injury and subsequent inaction
my muscles have faded slightly away

which perhaps is good

now I can't rely on them to prove my worth

I love the thickness of my limbs
how they swell beneath my shirt and jeans
express strength

but there must be a strength in the words I choose
for strangers and friends

when we drink in the pubs with tall windows

the breeze just barely lifting the curtains

chatter moving like a current

the life being formed

WHEN WARRINGTON WENT LOOKING FOR FRAMPTON

from the bell,
a blizzard to his head as thuds hissed

on swung gloves, dazed
I realised I was never a boxer. Never a boy

to hit jaws how he hits pads, heart
like Frampton who fires back from the ropes,

defiant.
There's a place for me in their gyms

at a bag,
shadowboxing far from their roped arena

by a mirror,
seasoning my physique with the idea of combat.

While boys slug it out, I work a body of air,
alone

to learn nothing
of how, after hooks crunch a cheekbone

pain thaws
to Frampton surviving the twelfth,

Warrington cradling his leaking forehead
with huge mitts,

ref gathering both fighters in his arms
like the remains of a brood.

BALANCE

I want to know if it's possible
to work too hard. My thoughts are trapped

like water in stone. Outside
the leaves

bristle in the sun. I've spent my life
at this table, working in this pool of light.

I promise I'm not looking for some obvious resolution
in which I open the window

to let a far off and symbolic laughter
drift in on the wind.

My life has been well lived, so far. I know everything
about how light fixes itself in the rim

of a pint glass. How to roll up a sleeve
just far enough

that the skin and bone of the elbow
press against the table in the beer garden.

UNDIMMED

an apricot sky seen alone is no less magic for being seen alone — Amy Key

again I am returning from a failed date

the lights of the northern line are cruel

in my best clothes I am exposed to their glare like a defeated boxer

whose once colourful shorts are now just sad

I don't think I am a lonely person

but still I sit across from strangers in pubs

seeking connection or life over a single candle

the light of the basement poking up through the floorboards

perhaps it's because now I am young and handsome and this will
          not always be true

perhaps it's the memory of other nights in other pubs with other girls

when there was no need for a candle

the glow between us already very much present

there was one who took me to her room and turned out the lights

I never spoke to her again and this guilt is now an ink that billows
       in my veins

it's billowing now in the harsh light of the underground where I
       sit alone

where I am telling myself I deserve this and knowing I am right

and perhaps I deserve it in a good way too

because as I return to my room and look out at the skyline at night

I see every crane and tower lit up with red as though the city is
       studded with rubies

I always thought I needed to share this jewelled view of the city
       with someone to make it real

WALKING IN POLESDON LACEY

among the autumn leaves all soaked in rain and light

copper, auburn

the crisp winds of noon

we're among the autumn leaves and yes

I am telling you about them

because this is the first time we have walked together

in the dazzling, rustling scene that everyone knows

and I am finding that I didn't know at all

TONIGHT I WANT TO LIVE AND

I am trying my best but still the evening trees are printed against
        the darkening blue

I want so much life from this city but every time I absorb this
        scene I feel ashamed

how many would kill for this darkening blue

how many have it and don't notice

how many want me to come into their lives

not me exactly but the idea of someone like me

how many have the idea of my life

tonight with its rain on the patio in the porch light

each drop as brief as the time I have with the moss on the brick wall

with the withered leaves that continue to scatter about the road

PETRICHOR

caught between separate times this evening

in the garden with the still-unflowered lavender

I wish I could hand this sadness back to the summer

leave myself in clear air

we sat out here on the decking

back when love, or the idea of love, was still enough

to sustain us. I am yet to think

of how the garden shines after rain

IMMERSION

After we fell apart, the water wasn't there to catch me
but to keep me moving forward.

Out here in the reservoir
I became as much a part of the air, wet patio and gulls
as the silky splashes in my ear, as the dinghies

that translate wind into motion by the opposite bank,

the reeds that nod like an ancient congregation.

When I turn my head for breath mid-stroke, I see light
trapped in water, in the brief crawl
of my arm like a blood.

You too would have fitted out here, which perhaps
would have solidified the disjoint between us.

Not for you these gulls, air and dinghies.

For you the sand and blue of a faraway beach.

I'm glad we hung a bridge across our crevasse. It feels okay
to call that love.

Out here the swimmers strip their wetsuits from their backs,
fling their sodden husks
over the railings, let the sun begin to heal.

Everyone as deep in this world out here
as a yolk.

GARDEN

I've woken at peace,
so it's important not to think. I return instead
to the familiar images: steam rising from the boiler
below the house, the pale leaves
on the tree whose name I never learned.
All I've ever done with these things
is try to know myself
through their movement in the garden; the way a branch
composes itself after a bird takes flight, or how the lamp
hung from the decking
will turn just so in the wind. All I am doing now
is understanding that the best way to ground myself
in this moment
is to pay attention to the green drops of bud
that have bled from the sycamore, the rain-soaked branches
of the trees, the heat
of my mug against my palm; it all keeps
the scenarios from my mind, the fractured many worlds
I move between, the same I suppose
as anyone, all of us just meeting from time to time
in this one (with the boiler steam
and morning wind) to pause and rest.

HUMAN LIGHT

Hornets are chewing on a crucifix, carrying the mulch in their mouths
to their nest, spreading it against the papery walls

the way I pretended to shake before the Lord
that night I stood in a big top tent,

surrounded by bodies that swayed
like wheat, a priest's arms raised above us all,

the drums and song of a Christian band blowing over us
in a breeze.

That year, I was desperate to belong, so I imagined a light
leaking out from my heart to my limbs, stood quivering into the prayers

until those around me placed their hands on my skin
and the lie moved between us like blood.

/

the day I almost died the hotel room was a mess

my brothers' holiday shirts were strewn about like wreckage

I sat in it all while my body inflamed from the peanuts in the cake

hives covered my skin like the work of many wasps

my throat a clenched fist

death as final as a wall

/

A girl, half my size, once propped me up
after my ankle snapped. This stranger, she walked with me,

stopping at every bench and post, until finally
the pain groped

like a vine. She knelt down in the middle of Oxford Street,
grasped my calf, closed her eyes and murmured.

/

the moment I almost died I thought of nothing but myself

my mum sprinting to the hotel desk for an ambulance was very
          much a separate person

sitting there dying among the towels the world went silent and hard

I was alone but in no way lonely

like a flower in concrete

I didn't think of hell

/

As she prayed, God,
I looked for you and felt hollow. The girl wouldn't have wanted this,
but it was the kindness of her hands on my leg,

not the thought of your moving between us,
that scattered a real light out
through my ribs.

/

how many cowards have been convinced they've gone to hell

I heard of one who during his twelve minutes of death claimed to
            have woken in a very dark room

woken with the feeling of being surrounded by chained bodies in
            the cold air

I always thought the fear of this room would return to me as I died

but all I could look at was my face in the hotel room mirror

swollen choking and mine

/

I once told a girl that I spend hours in the gym for myself,
not for her. I think I was right and wrong;

my body is my own,

but it should exist in relation to another,
like the glowing heads of two deep-sea fish
in the black.

/

I never saw the girl who prayed for my ankle again. She was tiny:
when she propped me up, I could feel her body trembling under
my weight. There was a togetherness between us. I think of what
she did so often. It was what a God would want her to do. My mum
told me she has faith because of the idea that no sin can push her
out of God's love; there's nothing she could do to make him stop
loving her. She loves me in spite of the plates I flung from the
table. Perhaps absence is the reality, like a child gliding on a bike,
unaware the father's hand is gone.

/

I think I was wrong, when I said I pretended to shake before God
as we worshipped in the big top tent. There was an element of
            pretence, but also

of blending: I remember every person around me becoming part
of a moment. The light and song held us together

in our faith, solidified us
in golden air.

/

Every year I slept through the Easter sunrise service. Mum would
                return
with photos of mist among trees, lit by the dawn
like scorched breath.

/

sometimes I feel a presence in the rain or below my skin

I bite back at my friends' easy hatred of preachers on the street

I know the warmth in the coffee cups distributed at my mum's church

in their rich tea biscuits and knot of cables on the stage

how Sunday mornings glowed like a torch for them

I know the cold of the houses they returned to

I remember visiting a friend's when I was very young

in their hallway was a framed photograph of their garden fence at night

light was moving like water on that fence with no apparent source

I can't remember the story exactly but they told me it was God

I can see now that the photo itself was light for them

I can feel now the photo becoming light for me

perhaps all that matters is that we have these miracles to kindle
     our chests

perhaps it's us perhaps it's God I don't know all that matters is
     that there is light

RESOLVE

to smell smoke the colour green and the heat of many bodies

to learn what the beat can teach my body about itself

the loosened arms all raised against the stage

what a canvas we make of this

the bass in my belly now what can it make of me

the aggression of it

I just want to feel the gold of it

there's not a dry hair in this room

the music in my chest as if the band has given me a new and brief
way to stay alive

to push myself down into the open moment in the knowledge it
won't last

my life will not become a trail of lost moments

I'll absorb them all

this year I allowed love

to pass out of me like a train

relearned the internal width of me

hollow for song

I'll fill myself with every noise

as if the birds are yet to sing

ACKNOWLEDGEMENTS

Thanks are due to too many people to name each person individually, but I'd like to thank everyone I've ever shared a workshop with, including those at the University of Manchester from 2015 to 2017, Julie Corbett's Stanza group in Hull, everyone on the UEA Poetry MA 2018/19, those in the various Poetry School groups in London and every person in every other group/course/class I've missed.

Thanks as well to everyone who has ever taught me poetry, in particular John McAuliffe, Tiffany Atkinson and Meryl Pugh.

Thanks to Aaron Kent at Broken Sleep Books for shepherding this pamphlet into the world and for his careful and considerate editing. Thanks as well to Molly Twomey for reviewing and editing this manuscript before I submitted it for publication.

Thank you to Amy Key for her kind permission to use a quote from her essay 'A Bleed of Blue' as the epigraph in the poem *undimmed*.

Thanks are due as well to the editors of the following publications, where some of these poems appeared for the first time: *Anthropocene*, *bath magg*, *Ink, Sweat and Tears*, *The Rialto* and *Poetry Wales*.

And special thanks to my family, all of whom taught me the values of hard work and compassion, qualities without which this pamphlet would never have been written. I love you all.

LAY OUT YOUR UNREST